Omni Consulting Firm Credit Course Book

For Class or Stand Only Users - Profitable for All

Joanna Walker-McClain

WESTBOW
PRESS®
A DIVISION OF THOMAS NELSON
& ZONDERVAN

WestBow Press books may be ordered through booksellers or by contacting:

WestBow Press
A Division of Thomas Nelson & Zondervan
1663 Liberty Drive
Bloomington, IN 47403
www.westbowpress.com
844-714-3454

ISBN: 978-1-6642-4215-9 (sc)
ISBN: 978-1-6642-4214-2 (e)

Print information available on the last page.

WestBow Press rev. date: 04/19/2022

INSPIRATION OF THIS BOOK

This book was written with the inspiration of God in dealing with credit in the bank and seeing many clients that would like to acquire credit and was not able to, due to the factors discussed in this book or series. Many could not, because of no established credit, not so good credit or other known factors. I did not want to see clients or an individual not able to get the credit they needed to get a home loan or a car loan or things of value and need; in the time they needed it.

Many times, if you don't know what's affecting the situation you are not able to get the answer to make a change or find the solution. This book helps you to understand credit, utilize credit at the times they are needed and how to add or get what you need to make a difference. A difference could be one small thing that can lead to huge success in your credit financial life. Understand, there's more to the picture than just credit- your finances are made up of many facets and credit happens to be a part of them. Everyone has to get credit – you can't get around it. To buy a house you need credit, unless you plan to buy it out right, and as a former Banker in the field for 14 years and a degree in Finance, I would say to you that's not the best and wisest choice, because that money of buying a house out right could be a huge investment in the investment market that will yield a great return and could pay off your house in 15 years on a 30 years mortgage with just using the interest earn and maybe a small portion of the principle or money invested. This journey in this course/class will teach you all these importance and how credit plays a factor into it. Is credit a bad thing – not at all – I would always recommend to the clients that I took care of in the bank, when you are offer it – take it,(credit cards, loans, anything credit) because you will never know when you will need it and then COVID-19 hits and all these came back to me -telling clients you may not need it now but the time may come when you will, at least you won't have to call the bank or go to the bank to apply or get it- you already have it and continue life as normal. Then came covid-19 and it took normality out of the banking world to where things are closed down or took away the way things were for a while. It's always great to have a credit card for emergency or Mr. Rainy Day. So, one needs to understand "as I will tell those clients – life happens – but there's a solution – let's find the best one for you." So, with that, not everyone financial status or needs are the same or look the same, one may need - $1,000,000 – if you are a corporation or in the business field – (depending on your business needs) or one may need just a small amount to make it happen. That could be a house loan, personal loan and all the other. This is an exciting course that teaches you the things that you need to understand to make a good financial decision before even touching the bank. As in this course, as noted, you share the story that you want the bank to read on your credit report. Come along with me and explore the many facets of life's financial choices from checking account to investment to credit. See, your finances are more than credit. Let's talk – what's your story.

CONTENTS

WEEK I

Different Elements of your finances
"Staying in control of your finances"

✓ Cash

- o   Checking accounts – Important
- o   Savings accounts – Daily savings easy access
- o   CDs – Another way to save – hard access
- o   Cash on Hand or pocket – Emergency, another easy access

✓ Credit

- o   Loans
- o   Lines of credit
- o   Credit Cards
- o   Just credit

- ✓ Investments
  - o IRAs (Roth & Tradition) – before and after taxes)
  - o 401K – Employer
  - o Home – Number 1 Investments
    - Loans and lines of credit – Cash access and most importantly borrowing from oneself

When in control of finances: benefits

- ➢ Purchase Timeshare
- ➢ Vacation Home purchase
- ➢ College investments
- ➢ Children
- ➢ Spoil oneself
- ➢ Business Ventures

Is control a bad word? – Trivia

Saying in control – budget or goal

Budget – a monthly tool use to stay on track of expenses. Income and expenses being look at more closely. Help you to keep all things accounted for.

Goal – A desire milestone or a purpose you want to reach or obtain.

One can have a goal to pay off their credit cards in a certain amount of time (months or years or even weeks). A goal is to keep one on track for a major purchase or self-accomplishment.

How does one stay on track with a budget and how about a goal?

What's your goal(s)?

Do you have a budget? Yes or No

Let's do one today

Income _____

Expenses

Rent or Mortgage _____

Phone _____

Water _____

Electric _____

Insurance _____

Credit cards _____

Credit Cards _____

Credit Cards _____

Car Note _____

TV _____

Misc(Food) _____

Misc(Gas) _____

Misc _____

Misc _____

Misc _____

Total Exp _____$

Income – Total exp= Net of what's left to spend

Notes of what learn:

Questions _

❋ Are you renting and can afford to own?

Market is good for shopping for a house – may be expensive, but a great time to purchase while rates are low. Market is rising in value.

❋ Is paying down credit cards in one personal loan the best way to go?

❋ Do you have an expense that needs to be refinance or look or shop for better rates?

I literally lower my car insurance by $300+ that was a huge savings, happy day.

❋ What short term goal can you make that can change your situation or current position and give you a brighter look on everything?

Sometimes it's changing one thing that can make everything better.

Homework:

Review your budget sheet we did today and see what makes sense to cut back on or refinance or let go.

Next week we look at what Creditors look for to make a loan to their customers or clients. Knowing what they are looking for will give you a head start of the approving process. Next week it's going to be fun.

Come ready to explore the 5 c's of credit.

WEEK 2

What does Creditors look for? "5 C's of Credit"

❋ Character – Payment history – your character to pay back

❋ Conditions – Reason for applying

❋ Capital – How much will you invest towards loan

❋ Collateral – Secure or unsecure -do you have a property or anything of value to secure the loan

❋ Capacity – Ability to repay – DTI (debt to income)

Let's take each piece by piece

Before we do – let's pull a copy of your credit report – Let's go to annualcreditreport.com. This will give you a sense of what's on your credit report and you can follow piece by piece.

Creditor's look at:

- ➢ Years of Credit
- ➢ Payment History
- ➢ Miss Payments
- ➢ Consistent with Credit
- ➢ Inquires – how often you pull your credit
- ➢ Balances on your accounts – especially your credit cards. These are unsecure and are weighted heavier than a house loan or even a loan that has a fixed monthly payment.
- ➢ Credit mix – do you have a variety of credit? – believe it or not – it's attractive to Lenders. Credit mix like credit card, mortgage, lines of credit, personal loans, cars, with a variety of cards like store cards, regular credit cards and other credit, are some if the credit mix that Lenders or Creditor look for.

➤ Length of time of the newest and the oldest card.

So, it's very important not to count yourself out, because I see sometimes that a person can have a high score and still declined for credit and another, a low score and can be approved. Each credit profile is individually base even though Lenders have a model to go by.

Any Questions?

We are going to go through each of the 5 c's of credit so a better understanding is obtained.

Leaving today – the goal is to understand credit, how to read credit and have a better handle of when to borrow and when to go for it.

Understanding what Creditors look for is taking advantage of your credit and staying in control of your finances.

✳ When you think about it, it's you borrowing from them and knowing how you are going to pay them back, in reality, they don't manage how you spend or borrow. You control what you borrow, what to spend and making your monthly payments. I see it as cash in a different way.

✳ Great use of credit is getting credit cards that rewards you for using their cards, like getting cash or points back, that is a wonderful way to motivate you to use that card and knowing that at the end of the year, it could be your way of getting gifts for one, two or even three persons.

Notes section:

_____

_____

_____

_____

_____

_____

_____

_____

<u>Tips to keep Handy:</u>

1. Never close out your first credit card or the longest account on your credit history

2. Keep payment on time – the great thing is you can use it again in the future

3. Check credit once a year – Experian have free credit pull as well.

4. Do a credit check to see if it's a good time to debt consolidate or refinance. It's like trading in a car because of too many miles on your car. See credit the same, the balances are getting high due to ____ and it's time to combine and lower payments, years and rates. Take advantage of all your savings.

5. If you own a house – A line of credit is a must. You are borrowing from yourself. Great way to do home improvements, new or used car purchase, my favorite – putting all your debt

against your home. Free up a lot of cash. Also great for whatever you want it to be for.

- It's your investment - take advantage.

- Your house can help you with vacation – whether buying a timeshare or paying off a timeshare.

- When you are ready, all you have to do is ask your bank for a line of credit. Once you can get it – ALWAYS get the most you can from your equity of your house. Sometimes persons goes for the lowest or even the need, but going for the max helps keep your credit healthy and score high.

- If you only take out what you want it's like maxing out a credit card, so always take advantage of getting the most you can. One of my passion credits instruments.

6. Try to keep credit utilization at 80% or lower. If you can go even lower that's very attractive to Lenders. How to calculate -take the limit

of your credit card and multiply it by 80% for example, a card of $10,000.00 * .80 = $8,000.00, so you should try not to go over $8,000.00 if it's possible. If you already have an idea or something coming soon and has to go more – go for it – it will balance out itself. So this is the way to look at 80%.

7. Never stop trying in getting it right, once you grab a hold to credit and how it's weighed it's a great tool to have in your wallet.

8. Keep a card or your line of credit for the unexpected events. Having a card just for unexpected or emergency keeps you ready for the unforeseen, for the most part.

9. Once you have all you need on credit – (credit cards, car, lines of credit/ loans and house), limit pulling your credit, pull like twice a year, so every 6 months, with the exception of when you buy a car or house, wait a year or so. Cars and house hit your credit the hardest and for

cars you may have more than one company hitting or bidding for your car loans. Dealership sends it out and go with the lowest interest rate of longest time depending on how long you requested. So, if you can go straight to your bank for credit for your car purchase it's the best way to go. This will help you on the long run. Know that through the dealership there will be more than one inquiry and inquires count against you and can hurt in the long run, depending on how soon you need to borrow. With your bank -it's one hit and more attractive to Lenders or Creditors.

10. To Creditors, pulling your credit back-to-back sends them a red flag and can be understandable if the bank you are borrowing from understand why that took place. However if not, they will see if as a negative.

11. Always know the reason outweighs everything else for Creditors. Healthy Credit is good and the way to go.

12. You are in the driver seat, so take control. Research, do loan checkups, look for the right time to do everything. Never procrastinate, it can hurt in the long run. So, when the opportunity present itself – GO FOR IT.

<u>Recap</u>:

Before you apply, look first at your score – if score is good, look at what's on your credit. Look at:

➤ Capacity – Can you take one more credit account? Most times it's best to debt consolidate

➤ Capital – Are you able to contribute if ask?

➤ Collateral – Do you have an asset like a car, house, anything of value that you have the title to (in a house _ equity) to secure the loan?

➤ Conditions – Do you have a good reason and explanation if ask for applying? Sometimes, the right lender may help you word it the right way to get to their underwriters. Relationship with a good institution goes a long way as well. Build one with the bank you have.

➤ Character – Do you have a good payment history?

All these five c's are what you are measure by when you go to apply for a loan. You can tell what your chances are before applying, by answering all these five c's. If credit is good and you just need a short-term loan (call personal loan) and you have the income to support, your chances are high in the approval zone.

If you have collateral, income and good credit (or can explain any issue with credit) for instance – you were a co- borrower and the owner of the loan did not make you aware of the late they have on your credit and you are able to show Creditors or Lenders that it was satisfy you stand a great chance of being approve. Know that it has to make sense to the Lenders before they give it to you.

For any bank or Creditors, they are looking at how well you managed your credit, how much credit you have, are your cards close to the limit and if the loan is to pay these off (if can get a little tricky but stay with it – again good credit and income will meet you in the middle). Also, they look to see if you are able to pay back what you have plus what you are asking for. Look at it as they checking you out. So, with everything, your credit file tells the story. So, give your creditors a good story to enjoy.

Individuals, businesses – you control your finances and what is out there, so treat this part with more care than you do cash.

WEEK 3

Take Charge of what's Yours

Now that we have learned about the different elements of your finances, what Creditors are looking for with the 5 c's of credit, now let's look at taking charge of each of these.

Questions before we dive into this week lesson.

Anything that you want to review or go back to?

Are we on course in understanding what's going on in this class?

Do you have a handle on these topics so far?

Taking charge of what's yours is knowing what's yours.

We explore additional items in last week course like payment history, length of credit, usage, but let's add some other items and expand on last week.

Other things to make sure you know what's on credit is your personal information.

Your personal information is important so make sure that it's correct, because any discrepancy can be a hold up or even a turn done in your application. If you are married, ensure/check to make sure it's reported correctly- it could raise a red flag.

This is where you get hands on and taking control.

Most times if you don't know what's holding you back from an approval or holding up an application, if can be on a repeat cycle, but knowing what's counting against you, give you an advantage for the next application.

Checking your credit is not just for the score, but to examine what's posting or showing on your credit.

Fine tooth – read everything even the insignificant because it can be significant.

<u>For instance</u>:

A late payment posting – is it true? did it occur? A late payment should only show if you were 30 days pass due. If not, challenge it. We'll discuss how you can challenge it.

Are there other factors showing that should not? Challenge it. It can boost your score from its current reporting and change your credit profile for the good. This opens up the door to get more credit offers.

Taking charge –

❖ Do you have accounts that you can pay down or pay off in two payments? Pay those off and free up cash for paying down or paying off other accounts.

❖ Always have a main card that you can easily pay off by a transfer or a payment. That card should be a card with your primary bank, where you can easily pay down for a purchase or use for an emergency item. Having a card with your primary bank is another way of taking control of what's yours. You can easily see what's happening, like balance on card, transaction posting and even requesting an increase if needs arise.

❖ Once credit is looking the way you want it to look to you and your Creditors, don't accept all offers. You have the power to say no, even if they are compelling.

❖ Double check to see if you have all you need for the future if any situation should arise. That means you have a daily or main card, you may have a second daily or main card and also you may have a card for emergency. (Before my business, I had 3 cards and for me that's all I needed, each card served a purpose; and other offers I would decline, because I had all I needed.

Then the business came and I needed now to add things for this need). I started looking for other cards to established the business and to get things going for the business. If you are a business owner you can read that in that section. After the business has all it needs, I will evaluate and use accordingly. But the great news is that being a business owner these new cards open up additional possibilities. So now I have what I need, but may eliminate the use.

❖ Cards are one element; do you have a home line of credit? First, do you own you own home? If so, what's stopping you from acquiring a line of credit if you don't have one? Know that you are borrowing from yourself. How so? Let's talk about it. So.............., who owns their own home or looking to? This is my favorite loans/ lines to talk about, because it's yours and you have the control of what you spend and use. It's fun, I mean it's fun to have.

❖ Just like a line of credit, do you have room to reward yourself? It maybe that you are looking and needing to have a new car but you are paying more out of pocket for car repairs and a low monthly payment on a car can surprise you. It just takes some re-evaluation on your budget. The new car will go a long way and probably provide you with a piece of mind and maybe that's what it takes to see everything differently. Each person story is different. What yours? Mine was the business.

Take some time to think on this. What can you change to make a future impact that you want to see? Sometimes it takes just a small adjustment. Once you come up with that and you want to do a one on one with me, we can do that. We have time to do some today (if in class session) or we can schedule at your best hours or time (for in class session or stand-alone purchasers) I am here for you.

The class is small so we can keep your personal information private. So, as I walk around, I will point on something that you may need to think about or discuss together. That could be a change that can make things different.

What else would you like to touch on?

This class is here to empower you and to help you take control of what's yours.

WEEK 4

Driving To Success

Now that we have cover taking control of what's yours and knowing how to read your credit report, you are now driving to success.

So, I am giving you all the keys to your credit report to drive to success. This next section is where you'll talk the most, and I'll listen and answer your questions.

Who wants to drive first?

In this section/class you can share any stories. Could be where you were before you came to class and how the class has empowered you and help to reach to this section of success. What will you do going forward and what will be your biggest and least thing to do with credit? It could also be I didn't know how close I was in everything.

Dress for this class – In suits- business. You really are going to feel the change in your attire. Empowerment is the key. Whether you are taking the course from home, in person or self-study, dress for this section. It's going to lead you into great opportunities and help you to see things more clearly as you are driving to success. You have learnt the secret to credit and understanding what your Creditors or Lenders are looking for. So even when you show up to apply – dress for any business transaction. They should see and know they are dealing with someone that has control over their finances and know why they are seeking their lending service today and know that you will pay back even sooner. When that session is over of meeting or talking to a Lender, leave an impression that they want to see you back and want to earn more of your business. Let them be the one to work for your business and not you working to show them that you are capable with character, collateral, conditions and capital to make it happen. Have them to the edge of their seats wondering what a session and who are you. You write the story for your Lenders and Creditors to read. Understand that you have many tools to managing your finances, credit just happen to be a part of the mix and a small piece. So, leave them guessing and intrigue. Manage your cash well, manage a savings account, manage a checking account and grow into a cd and IRA for the future retirement years of your life. Open and explore all the possibilities of managing your finances and as a former banker in that field for nearly 14 years only a month shy – I have worked form a Customer Service helping individual accounts as well as business accounts. I have worked the line of the tellers helping those check cashers and clients making a deposit or other banking activities to becoming a manager and helping grow three offices and being able to be in the market and helping small business clients grow. God has equipped me and make me a diverse banker in my days and now using those skills and all that he taught me and show to empower others to grow. Many don't get the counseling in the bank on credit and your finances, unless someone really take the time to see beyond the scope of the screen and what you have, to knowing you and finding ways to make it happen. These tools are here to help you in all walks of life. I am your Creditor Counselor to help you get it started and to succeed. You have not really succeeded unless you know how to do it – that means if the banks are close – you are not shut off to your finances and managing it. Who better to be a great financial person than you knowing what's yours, taking charge to a brighter future? You are to be able with your Advocate, (if you should have one) to know what's happening till it becomes a second nature. Driving to success is not only in your credit but remembering the beginning topic in the first week of the class - different elements of your finances. All these equates the success that you are looking for and to have.

Interactive class

We may have groups, come ready for anything.

WEEK 5

Now You Are On Your Way

The journey to learning and understanding credit from this class has come to an end, but a new start for something great for all of you. It's celebration class but we are going to do some recap just in case you have any questions.

You have conquered the fear of knowing and want to look at your credit and to see it's just a tool to get you in front of the right lenders or creditors. If you are planning on starting a business, you'll need this class and now you have it (also, OCF will offer another class for business). Keep your credit looking good, knowing what's on it and happening and don't be afraid to say no or to challenge it.

You are on your way to financial success and that's knowing what you have, what is missing and where you want to be. Once you are there, keep evaluating once a year to see if you are on the right page.

Also, look for the best deal that is out there: like insurance review, loans refinance for mortgage and any loans and add or take away what's not needed.

Make the best choice for you or you and your family or you, family and your business. It must look right and make sense. Success of your credit and other elements are in your hands. Remember its what you say – you are in control of your finances.

Have a mix of everything:

* ❋ Cash on hand
* ❋ Checking account – the lowest amount should be in your checking
* ❋ Saving account – the next highest

* Cds – have a mix – terms should vary from short terms to long term
* Investments – If it makes sense. Look at rates, term and the market. Always check to see what the market is doing.
* Loans – like your line of credit and I am going to share a story.

I know a person that works and has a 401K and also a line of credit. How did he make the most of his work and his house? He uses is line of credit he had against his house and pay back as he goes; but he uses his income as an invest stream and invest the most into his 401k, that when he was ready to retired, he had established himself, because his house allows him to invest more than the company match and got the most back to the retirement and uses his line as an everyday use and living lifestyle, like having a beach house and uses it also as a rental property. You have the power to borrow from yourself while allowing your work to do the most investing for you. Don't fall in the trap of others that say when your house is paid off – let it be. That's the time to put it to use.

Improve the value of your home with home improvements by borrowing from yourself. As we mentioned in the above, different ways to use your line of credit. So many important attractions to having a line of credit.

You can do the same, but remember every person story is different.

My business cards are right here for you when you need to reach out by email (jamaicangal43@aol.com or jesusbaby071995@gmail.com) or by a phone call (540-471-6452). Please keep in touch and I will do same. For all purchasers that may need help in going through the material, please contact me at the information provided. I'll check in to see how you are doing and that you are not alone. If anything comes up, come see me or reach out in whatever way is best.

WRAP UP

This course has come to an end and hope this journey has taught you a lot and affirmed what you may not have known. Take the skills from this course and empower yourself and others to be great and do great. Teach your children or other family members. Share the information and let's spread the good about what this course can do for one's future. Let's empower as many as we can. It's all about spreading the love and empowering to make the world a better place. This will help to ease those who may be frustrated of not able to do what they want because their situation may look like it's the end and no help, but in this course, it will help and can help everyone. This is one level, and maybe your level to move forth, or another level in having expansion on the material for further understanding and that you can do by reaching out by email or phone and taking it another level in knowing you have a full understanding, this is for those who just purchase and did not take the class.

Here's to a successful future.

Change lives.

ABOUT THE AUTHOR

Joanna Walker McClain is a Former Banker for 14 years and served in different areas in the Banking Institute. Her goal is to teach as led by the Holy Spirit to empower lives and to change situations according to the Lord's directions. Credit is a topic that she has worked with a lot and is ready to pass on to see others successful.